PENGUIN BOOKS
JAMES DEAN REVISITED

Born in New York City in 1928, Dennis Stock began his photographic apprenticeship with Gjon Mili in 1947 and, since 1951, has
been associated with Magnum Photos, Inc. One-man exhibitions
of his work have been shown at the Chicago Art Institute, which
has purchased his pictures for its permanent collection, and at gal-
leries and museums in Zurich, San Francisco, Tokyo, and New
York City. In addition to *James Dean Revisited*, books by him
include *Jazz Street*, *California Trip*, *California the Golden Coast*,
and *The Circle of Seasons*. Mr. Stock now lives in Woodstock,
New York.

James Dean Revisited

Text and photographs by

DENNIS STOCK

Penguin Books

For Marcus and Ortense Winslow

Penguin Books Ltd, Harmondsworth,
Middlesex, England
Penguin Books, 625 Madison Avenue,
New York, New York 10022, U.S.A.
Penguin Books Australia Ltd, Ringwood,
Victoria, Australia
Penguin Books Canada Limited, 2801 John Street,
Markham, Ontario, Canada L3R 1B4
Penguin Books (N.Z.) Ltd, 182–190 Wairau Road,
Auckland 10, New Zealand

First published in the United States of America in simultaneous hardcover
and paperback editions by The Viking Press and Penguin Books 1978
Reprinted in Penguin Books 1979

LIBRARY OF CONGRESS CATALOGING IN PUBLICATION DATA
Stock, Dennis.
James Dean revisited.
1. Dean, James, 1931–1955—Portraits, etc.
2. Moving-picture actors and actresses—United
States—Portraits. I. Title.
PN 2287.D33s7   791.43′028′0924 [B]   78-16255
ISBN 0 14 00.4939 8

Printed in the United States of America by
Halliday Lithograph Corporation, West Hanover, Massachusetts
Set in Memphis

ACKNOWLEDGMENT
The New York Times: "Another Dean Hits the Big League" by Howard Thompson.
Copyright © The New York Times Company, 1955. Reprinted by permission.

Introduction

New York, 1943

The day was filled with pain. Could Cagney, Bogart, or Tracy erase my thoughts? In the morning the doctors declared my father's illness critical. By afternoon he was dead. That evening I disappeared into the black cavity of the neighborhood movie theater, where I hoped the power of the giant screen would draw my mind away from the unbearable hurt of severance and guilt. It seemed that the finality of death need not cripple if illusion could spirit my feelings into the world of celluloid. That was my perspective at fifteen.

Many of us turn to films for alleviation. As a boy I spent a great many of my summers in the cool darkness of the corner theater. The stars, stories, and locations transported me into fantasies far richer than the reality of the ghetto. It seemed as if Hollywood were heaven and it could heal; time and experience have taught me the opposite.

Fairmount, Indiana, 1955

After the death of my friend James Dean, few illusions about the paradise of Hollywood remained. In the face of the reality of his austere funeral, all fantasies attached to the world of stars were greatly reduced.

Lew Bracker and I had arrived late at the simple brick Quaker church in Fairmount. Family and friends were already seated in the straight-backed pews. At the head of the center aisle, in front of the altar, lay the closed coffin, bedecked with flowers. For all I knew, it was the same coffin he had foolishly posed in a few months before. The organ played "Goin' Home." We found seats finally in the front row to the left of the altar. I immediately saw gentle Marcus Winslow, Jimmy's uncle. The family sat diagonally across from the coffin. Our eyes met often, and we had great difficulty choking back the sobs of pain we shared. It had been less than eight months since my last visit to Fairmount, with Jimmy, when I had had the pleasure of staying with the family as I photographed and pursued Jimmy's origins. We had hit it off exceptionally well, for the Winslows were extremely open and gracious. It seemed so wrong that this decent, generous family had to suffer this untimely loss. As surrogate parents, their devotion to Jimmy's upbringing was complete, their love unlimited.

I don't remember the eulogies; the wounds of loss blurred most of what was said. The service completed, the family filed out to receive the condolences of Fairmount friends. Hesitantly, I approached Marcus and we fell into each other's arms. "Boy, where have you been?" His face was tear-drenched and desperate. His wife, Ortense, admonished me for not having contacted them sooner, but was grateful that I had been the catalyst in releasing Marcus's repressed feelings. He had been silent since the notification of Jimmy's death. Marcus, the farmer, and Dennis, the city slicker, were as close as two people could get at that moment. Our mutual love of Jimmy and respect for each other helped to alleviate our devastation. My fondness for the Winslows remains intact to this day.

When I look back at Los Angeles in the early fifties, and specifically Sunset Boulevard, it reminds me of the board game in which you try to move clockwise and upward, past designated obstacles, into "Stardom and Wealth." Rolling the dice at the start, as a visitor on Mexican downtown Alvaro Street, the player inches past the pastel bungalows of Old

Hollywood. With many other aspirants, we come to a holding pattern at the crossroads of Crescent Heights and Sunset. This intersection marks the beginning of the infamous Sunset Strip. If the dice were good, the roller continued and was hurled into the status-filled setting of Beverly Hills. A jump or two more and the ultimate was at hand: a sunset-bathed beach house. This road was literally and figuratively bumpy, curved and highly deceptive. Till this day, few participants reach the Pacific enclave of the stars. Those who do are usually badly scarred and bruised.

The Sunset Strip in the fifties (I doubt if it has changed much) was the battlefield for those who needed to conquer Hollywood. In this two-mile area of nightclubs, restaurants, strip joints, and agents' offices the struggle for recognition was fought. Starlets, directors, producers, and actors elbowed one another for the space of two brief lines in the trade gossip columns. The establishments on the strip thrived on the anxiety of the fame-seekers, catering to the illusion of success; the prices were high, the façades ornate. Waiting at the foot of the strip for their turn were contestants who lived in the romantic hotels and cottages of the bygone twenties.

Those who arrived from the disciplines of the Broadway environment tried to make as gentle a transition into Hollywood as possible. They lived in the symbolic settings of the Chaplin and Keaton era, the Château Marmont and the Garden of Allah. The aging bungalows and suites insulated the ambivalent seekers from the East. The coffeeshops, diners, and drugstores were commandeered by the less affluent and served as social centers for the New York crowd. It was in this surreal, intense atmosphere that I met James Dean for the first time.

As an already established photojournalist in Hollywood, I had access to stars and movie events. On Sundays it was customary for Nicholas Ray, the director, to hold soirées at his bungalow on the grounds of the Château Marmont. Nick, an East Coast maverick, did not host singularly social affairs but rather offered the opportunity for talented people to meet weekly, exchange ideas, and form new ties. People from every part of the film industry converged on his little white bungalow on Sunday afternoons in the winter of '54-'55. The jugs of wine and the heated discussions somewhat reduced the superficiality that we experienced the rest of the week on the sound stages and in the offices of Hollywood. Amid the animation of gesturing hands and passionate discussions, I stood somewhat removed and shy; like most photographers, one foot in and one foot out. Nick noticed my reserved appearance and led me up the small flight of stairs to a corner where a young man reclined, in a mood that seemed similar to mine.

We both awoke to the moment of our host's gracious introductions. I, the photographer, was presented to James Dean, the actor, and with that, Nick departed. There was nothing terribly imposing about this bespectacled young man. At first, his responses to my brief inquiries and observations were monosyllabic. But as the wine flowed more abundantly, so did our conversation. Relaxed, Jimmy asked about different aspects of photographic techniques, and I happily obliged as best I could. Inevitably the conversation touched on his work, and on his most recent job. In a casual way he mentioned having completed a film with Elia Kazan called *East of Eden*; I drew a blank, for I had neither read the book nor heard trade rumors about the production.

We didn't pursue the film any further, but shortly before our conversation ended Jimmy invited me to attend a sneak preview of *East of Eden* the following Wednesday at a Santa Monica theater. With a nod and an "I'll see you there," we parted.

Midweek, I went to the shabby neighborhood movie house, totally unprepared for an experience that initiated a major chapter in my life. Jimmy's unassuming manner at Nick's had ill prepared me for the brilliant performance I experienced that night in *East of Eden*.

There are ailments that medicine will never cure. During adolescence feelings are uniquely intense and repressed, and we ache with inarticulation and emotional frustrations. The teenager wrestles for years with the "need to be understood." It is a logical challenge along the course to individuality. The searching society seeks symbols that universalize experience. The artist seeks order, instinctively, and often crystallizes through gesture or deed a universal truth. His perception reaches the very heart of our common experience, and identification is immediate for the viewer. We then acknowledge the brilliance of the symbol. This is art, and the

rarity of universal art makes James Dean's first
major film performance all the more extraordinary.
In *East of Eden*, as young Cal, who struggles to
communicate with an intransigent father he loves,
Dean expressed hues and shadings of adolescence
that had probably never been seen before. I and the
movie audience clearly empathized with Cal as
Dean led us masterfully through his plight of aliena-
tion and innocence. Capitalizing on the limits of the
adolescent's ability to articulate, Dean used his body
to the utmost. His expressions were exceptionally
graphic. Literally on the edge of my seat throughout
the screening, I mentally photographed his rich variety of powerful gestures.

There was no question that a star was born
with the first public screening of *East of Eden*, for the
entire audience applauded loudly as the house
lights signaled the end. It took a few moments for
me to reconcile the image of Cal with that of the un-
imposing, reserved young man of the previous Sunday night. What I knew was that I had to do a story on
James Dean. Out on the street, I searched for Jimmy
to congratulate him and to arrange for an early
meeting to discuss the possibilities of a photo essay.

In the alley on the side of the theater I found Jimmy seated on his motorcycle. He peered through his glasses at the crowds of newly acquired admirers; at this distance he could observe without being observed. Jimmy must have sensed his triumph, for as I approached, he burst into a big grin and said, "What do you think?" Since I was still deeply enveloped in the film, I simply blurted, "You are an outstanding actor!" We were interrupted by friends congratulating Jimmy, and I suggested we meet the following morning for breakfast.

Let me try to explain my own position and attitude as a young man in Hollywood in those days. My contacts with New York magazines were well known to many publicity-seeking actors and agents, so I had ample opportunity to meet as many famous and creative people as I wanted. And though I greatly enjoyed being in the presence of recognized creative people, I was also aware that the relationship could be parasitical if I did not photograph in meaningful ways but simply relaxed with the exclusive opportunities I had to cover stars and up-and-coming stars. Dull photographs of famous people often are acclaimed primarily because of the status of the subject, so I tried to pursue themes that were best stated by a multiple-picture essay. In each assignment I searched for depth and meaning. It made the possibility of an exceptional photograph more frequent. If the photograph was good in spite of the subject, I felt I had succeeded.

Breakfast took place at Googie's, on the strip, one of Jimmy's favorite hangouts. The coffeeshop was packed, as usual, with unemployed actors and actresses, exchanging trade gossip and reading *Variety* in search of leads to film castings. Jimmy arrived at nine, sat down, and before our conversation could begin, he was surrounded by admirers. The exceptional success of the previous night's "sneak" was the topic of conversation throughout the restaurant. For two hours Jimmy reigned supreme. Acquaintances tried to ingratiate themselves with exaggerated compliments as they jockeyed for a closer friendship with the rising star. My patience was running thin, and I indicated I was going to leave, since there was no chance to talk. In one swift move Jimmy leaped from our booth, paid the bill, and led me to his motorcycle in the parking lot. "Get on; let's go up into the hills. My agent's got a place up there with a beautiful view, and we can talk." Since I'd never ridden on a motorcycle, I mounted the Triumph with trepidation, and with the realization that I was being tested. It was the first of my tests. We sped up the winding roads of Laurel Canyon, my arms securely wrapped around Jimmy's waist. We leaned wildly at each curve in the road. I tightened my grip around Jimmy's heavy leather jacket and screamed above the roaring motor, "If I go, you go!" Finally we slowed down as we reached the section of the dry Hollywood hills where Dick Clayton's house was. Stretched below us was a goodly portion of Los Angeles, and, in the far distance, the Pacific. On the bare ground we sat and talked for five hours.

There was no question that our meeting was investigatory in nature. Sparingly, Jimmy volunteered information about his background, and I elaborated on my qualifications and credentials. His awareness of my friendship with Humphrey Bogart and my membership in the elite photo agency Magnum helped to further the idea of a collaboration. My intent was solely to lead the conversation back to

Jimmy's past so that I could start to formulate an outline of situations that we could visit and document with the camera. The story, as I explained it, was to reveal the environments that affected and shaped the unique character of James Byron Dean. We felt a trip to his hometown, Fairmount, Indiana, and to New York, the place of his professional beginnings, would best reveal those influences. We agreed to a trip to both those locales in the not too distant future. As was customary in my business, I would solicit an assignment guarantee to cover expenses. The obvious magazine to approach was *Life*. If I was assigned by the *Life* editors, we could set up a schedule for visiting Indiana and New York. We further agreed that I would have the first exclusive rights to a picture story on Jimmy.

It took only a week for *Life* to approve the assignment. I notified Jimmy, and we tentatively set our departure for Indiana and New York for two weeks hence. Meanwhile, I made a point of socializing a great deal with Jimmy, for the more I knew about his moods, the easier it would be to anticipate gestures and situations. By now there was an ever-increasing interest in the new star as the press became more and more aware of *East of Eden*. The upshot of Jimmy's increasing popularity was reflected in the new stipulations he tried to enforce on the *Life* coverage. At one point he insisted on a cover guarantee and the hiring of a friend of his to write the text. It was an unusual and highly egocentric gesture. I said I'd pass the request on to the editors. It was a foolhardy demand, which I never conveyed to the magazine, gambling on our growing friendship to keep the assignment afloat. I told Jimmy the editor's answer was no. For days he acted like a spoiled kid, and then finally came around, making it possible for us to leave for Fairmount the first week in February, 1955.

For Jimmy it was going home. But it was also the realization that the meteoric rise to fame that had already begun that night in Santa Monica had cut him off forever from his small-town Midwestern origins, and that he could never really go home again. Still, in those bitter-cold late-winter days, as Jimmy and I roamed the town and farm and fields of Fairmount, visiting family and friends, I came to know, or at least to glimpse, the real James Dean.

Fairmount, Indiana

By the time we arrived at Fairmount, Indiana, shooting on *East of Eden* had been completed but the film had not yet been released. Still, the townspeople sensed that James Dean was somebody special. The local papers had followed his blooming career; he had already appeared on television. But as yet no one suspected the full proportions his fame would assume.

Seated around the dining-room table in the Winslows' farmhouse in Fairmount are (clockwise) Jimmy, with back to camera; Charlie Dean, Jimmy's grandfather; Marcus Winslow, his uncle; Ortense Dean Winslow, his aunt; grandmother Emma Dean; and Markie, Jimmy's cousin.

Jimmy's parents moved to California when he was six. Three years later, on July 14, 1940, his mother, Mildred Dean, died of cancer. His father, a dental technician, stayed on in California, but Jimmy was sent back to Indiana to be brought up by his aunt and uncle, Ortense and Marcus Winslow, in Fairmount, where Jimmy's grandparents also lived. It is probable that Jimmy never got over his mother's death, but it is nonetheless hard to imagine a better home, for a boy in such a situation, than the Winslows'. They were Quakers, and as Jimmy's grandmother Emma once said of them, "Both are wise and gentle. Theirs is like a Quaker home should be. You never hear a harsh word there."

Jimmy's return to Fairmount was more than a mere visit. With the completion of *East of Eden* Jimmy had experienced Hollywood and the intimations of stardom. At this point he was straddling two worlds—the world of his origins in Fairmount and the early stages of stardom—and he knew instinctively that the two were in conflict. And so he went back to Fairmount, to examine his origins and to preserve what was relevant.

Unbeknownst to his family, Jimmy had a wire tape recorder strapped to him, with a microphone on his wristwatch. He probed Charlie and Emma about his background. Among the things they tried to figure out was where Jimmy got his theatrical flair. The only clue Charlie came up with was that one ancestor had been an auctioneer. One factor they didn't discuss, which certainly was pertinent, was that as a child Jimmy used to play theater with his mother. They had built a stage, and they would make up plays, which they then would perform with little dolls.

If you want to get to your roots, you go into graveyards, especially in a small town. One morning Jimmy, Markie, and I wandered through Fairmount's Park Cemetery, which was filled with many Dean ancestors, and suddenly happened on the gravestone of Cal Dean, who I believe was an uncle or a great-uncle. Both Jimmy and I were struck by the odd coincidence of the name, for Jimmy, of course, had just finished portraying Cal Trask in *East of Eden*.

February is a rough month in the Midwest—not the ideal time to observe anything, much less to probe your past. It is a lean, gray time, and that is the mood, too. But maybe this was part of Jimmy's constantly testing everything: nothing ought to be idyllic. As was so often the case with Jimmy, he seemed to stack the cards against himself.

Jimmy slid into a very simple and uncomplicated relationship
with Markie—somewhat as an older brother might. While he
was in Fairmount he helped Markie build a model Jaguar and
repair his bicycle, and on occasion played with him in his
improvised Soap Box Derby racer. I think Jimmy was seeing
himself as a young boy: Markie's childhood was so much like
his own, so intimately involved with the movement and
power of tractors. And from that you move on to bikes and
motorcycles and racing cars: the mechanical life. It was very
easy for Jimmy to adapt almost immediately to that facet of
the farm and, in that regard, to identify with his cousin.

Jimmy with his uncle Charlie Knowland.

In Martin Carter's motorcycle shop, where Jimmy bought his first motorcycle.

WE MUST GET HOME

We must get home! How could we stray like this?—
So far from home, we know not where it is,—
Only in some fair, apple-blossomy place
Of children's faces—and the mother's face—
We dimly dream it, till the vision clears
Even in the eyes of fancy, glad with tears.

We must get home—for we have been away
So long, it seems forever and a day!
And O so very homesick we have grown,
The laughter of the world is like a moan
In our tired hearing, and its song as vain,—
We must get home—we must get home again! . . .

The rows of sweetcorn and the China beans
Beyond the lettuce-beds where, towering, leans
The giant sunflower in barbaric pride
Guarding the barn door and the lane outside;
The honeysuckles, midst the hollyhocks,
That clamber almost to the martin-box. . . .

We must get home; and, unremembering there
All gain of all ambition otherwhere,
Rest—from the feverish victory, and the crown
Of conquest whose waste glory weighs us down.—
Fame's fairest gifts we toss back with disdain—
We must get home—we must get home again!

We must get home again—we must—we must!—
(Our rainy faces pelted in the dust)
Creep back from the vain quest through endless strife
To find not anywhere in all of life
A happier happiness than blest us then. . . .
We must get home—we must get home again!

*James Whitcomb Riley was the poet of the Hoosier, and Jimmy
loved to read from his work, which he did one day for me after
dinner, to give me a feeling of the people and place whence
he had come.*

"Tintype with Sow." Why? There is no logic to it, at least no logic readily apparent to the two young men Jimmy and I were then. When we speak of a tintype we usually think of a portrait or a family image. And family means where we come from, what we belong to. It seems apparent to me now that here Jimmy was testing the simplest of things: do I belong to the animals—to the pigs, the cattle, the goats? Do they accept me? It soon became clear that the barnyard animals easily accepted Jimmy, and he them. Don't underestimate that tintype with sow! A sow can be ferocious, and doesn't easily lend itself to the mad pose you see here.

The barnyard was a natural for Jimmy; he explored and performed in the pens, troughs, and barn, testing his past pleasures for their validity in the future. He appreciated the surreal aspects of our search and happily responded to the pigs' oinking accompaniment to the bongos, the sows' dignified pose for the portrait, and the blasé heifers' acceptance.

THE OLD HAYMOW

The Old Haymow's the place to play
Fer boys, when it's a rainy day!
I good 'eal ruther be up there
Than down in town, er anywhere!

When I play in our stable-loft,
The good old hay's so dry an' soft,
An' feels so fine, an' smells so sweet,
I 'most ferget to go an' eat.

From *The Complete Poetical Works of James Whitcomb Riley*, Grosset & Dunlap, 1937.

Jimmy carried his bongo drums with him wherever he
went—to New York, to Hollywood, and home to Fairmount.
He became more and more attached to them as he learned to
play better, and, as we've seen, he tried them out on the
barnyard animals. He tried them out on Markie, too, and
Markie's reaction was to clap his hands to his ears.

Jimmy in a real down-home pose, in his long johns.

We found an old Victrola down in the basement with some old 78s, and played them one afternoon.

The Sweethearts Ball was held on Valentine's Day, 1955.
Since Jimmy was in town, he was invited, and he not only
came but brought his bongo drums as well. During the evening he played with the band, and at one point gave a little
speech. He was at that time twenty-four, several years out of
school, but most of that year's seniors remembered him, and
now that word of his impending fame had reached Fairmount, requests for autographs seemed appropriate.

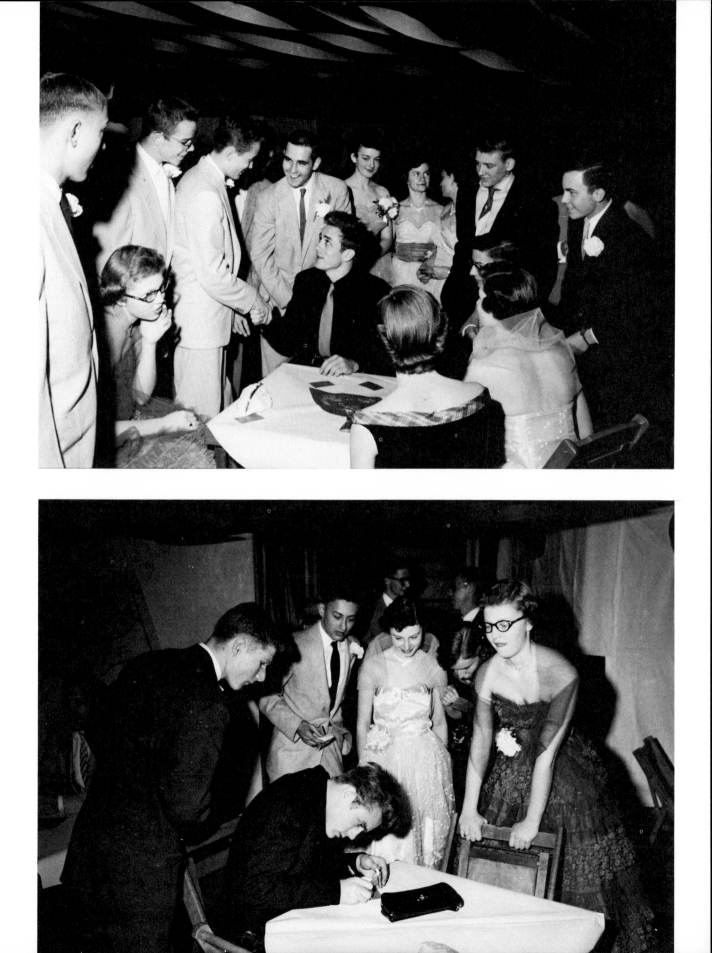

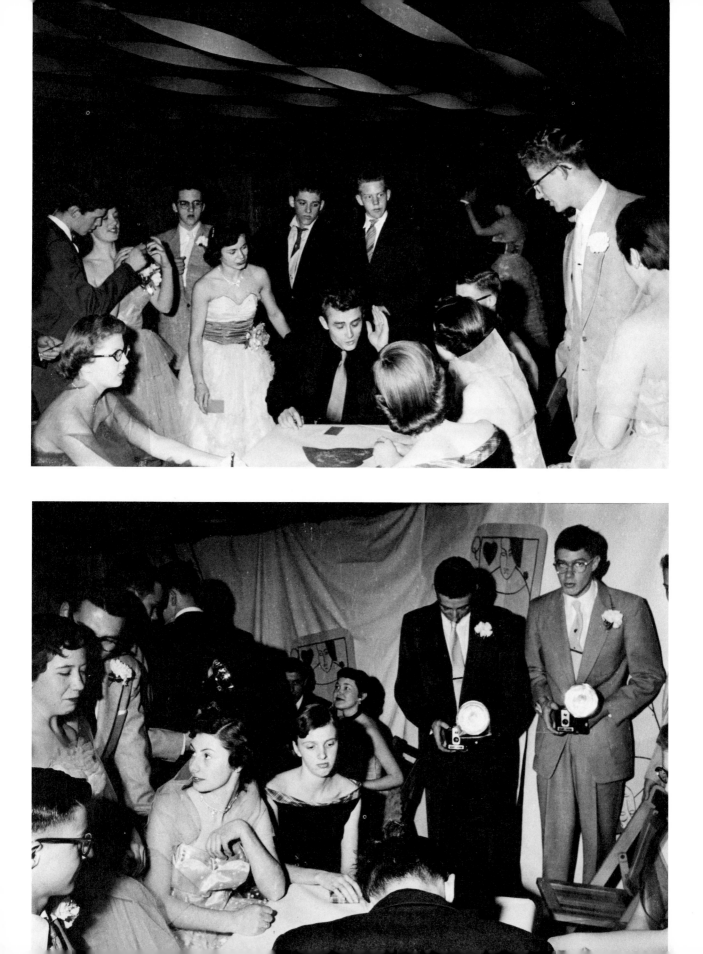

The old classroom.

Jimmy on the stage where he first performed.

Adeline Nall, Jimmy's high-school teacher and dramatic coach, who was responsible for getting him started in drama and forensic competitions. Jimmy won a number of state prizes for drama, debating, and elocution.

63

New York

Times Square. Jimmy haunted it. For a novice actor, in the fifties, New York was the place to go. Theater was thriving, and television was alive and well. The Actors Studio, directed by Lee Strasberg, was in its heyday. So when James Whitmore, Jimmy's first drama coach in Los Angeles, said to him, "Go East, young man," he went. And in many ways, Jimmy felt more at home in New York than in L.A.

He was not at all fastidious about his looks; in fact, he would turn up more often than not in shaggy-dog style at meetings both formal and informal. What prompted him to walk into this barber shop near Times Square one day when we were out walking I cannot say.

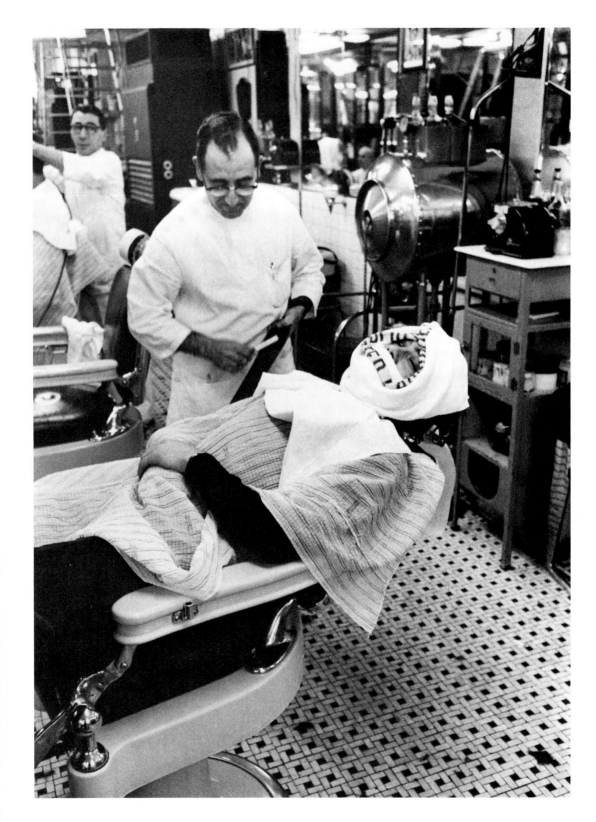

We used to roam the streets of New York together, and I liked to photograph Jimmy observing others. He had a great natural curiosity about people, was a collector of street vignettes, and I was forever amazed at the oddities he would stumble on to. One of the oddest was Jimmy's passing a store one day and pausing to see what one of the two little girls had in her hand. What was it? A chicken head. Only Jimmy would happen upon such surreal situations.

Jimmy had attended Lee Strasberg's classes at The Actors Studio before Elia Kazan tapped him to play Cal in *East of Eden*. ("Dean *is* Cal," Kazan is reported to have said after seeing Jimmy, and John Steinbeck was quick to agree.) Whenever Jimmy came back to New York, he would renew his links with The Actors Studio. Careful observers will doubtless be able to pick out of this 1955 photograph several other actors who subsequently went on to fame and fortune. This is a rare picture in every sense of the term, for Strasberg almost never let anyone photograph his classes.

Jimmy also studied dance as part of his actor's training. I am tempted to say this shows how seriously Jimmy took his art, which he did, but the fact is he was a dabbler: the bongo drums, African jazz, dance. Here he works out in Katherine Dunham's class, which was where he met Eartha Kitt.

Jimmy and Geraldine Page were good friends, and they used to get together often to talk shop, or just for small talk. Note that in the picture on the right Geraldine has a clipping of Jimmy—a prerelease article on *East of Eden*—hanging on her dressing-room mirror.

It seems that Jimmy's life in New York revolved around a very narrow area of a few blocks, the center of which was Times Square. I've often speculated that Jimmy's preoccupation with the drums was more an interest in sound than in the instrument itself: drums, motorcycles, sports cars—all vibrated with a powerful sound to which he responded.

Here he takes a drum lesson with Cyril Jackson, in a studio not far from Times Square.

Jerry's Bar on West Fifty-fourth Street, across from the old Ziegfeld Theatre, was one of Jimmy's favorite New York hangouts. Don't assume he's passed out because he's had too much beer. Jimmy was an insomniac—the worst I've ever met—so at odd times and in odd places he would simply pass out, for a few minutes or a few hours, then wake up and set out again. He lived like a stray animal; in fact, come to think of it, he *was* a stray animal. He had a couple of favorite spots on the East Coast, and two or three more on the West Coast. In New York he kept his fifth-floor walk-up apartment on West Sixty-eighth Street, but since he couldn't sleep, he spent relatively little time there.

Jimmy's insomnia posed a special problem for me: *Life* had
assigned me to do a possible cover of Jimmy, and I made
several appointments to shoot him. Sometimes he didn't show
up at all, and when he did, he'd look like utter hell—a two-
or three-day growth of beard, and enormous bags under his
eyes. He was only twenty-four, but the effects of his life-style
were already beginning to show.

We were walking down Sixth Avenue and suddenly Jimmy spied a furniture store near Rockefeller Center. "Performers are always being looked at," he said. "I wonder what it feels like to be inside and look out. Stay outside and photograph people's reaction to me just sitting there staring out. . . . "

How did people react? Most did notice him but then moved on. The point is, few people did react: this is New York, and the tempo of the city in the fifties was just about as fast as it is today. In a small town things would have been different, but in New York . . .

85

Howard Thompson, of The New York Times, *interviewing Jimmy at the apartment of his East Coast agent, Jane Deacy, just after* East of Eden *had opened at the Astor Theatre in New York.*

[*The New York Times*, March 13, 1955]

ANOTHER DEAN HITS THE BIG LEAGUE

By HOWARD THOMPSON

JAMES DEAN is the young man who snags the acting limelight in "East of Eden," which arrived at the Astor last week. Its opening has started a lively controversy over his histrionic kinship with Marlon Brando—and his professional competence. At any rate, 25-year-old Dean, a product of an Indiana farm, Hollywood, television and Broadway, has made an impression and now owns a Warner Brothers contract.

Count his supporting chore in last season's "The Immoralist" as having threefold significance insofar as this rapid rise is concerned. It netted him the Donaldson and Perry awards and, indirectly, the attention of director Elia Kazan, then scouting leads for "Eden," and finally, his flourishing reputation for unvarnished individuality. In a recent chat at his agent's apartment, west of the Yorkville area, Dean gave ample evidence that he was prepared to maintain that individuality.

He sat quietly, awaiting the first query. The slender frame and boyish features suggested a Booth Tarkington hero. The black corduroy shirt and trousers and a penetrating neutrality of expression, magnified by large, steel spectacles, did not. Had he caught "Eden" yet?

"Sure, I saw it," came the soft, abstract reply. His verdict? "Not bad."

"No, I didn't read the novel. The way I work, I'd much rather justify myself with the adaptation rather than the source. I felt I wouldn't have any trouble—too much, anyway—with this characterization once we started because I think I understood the part. I knew, too, that if I had any problems over the boy's background, I could straighten it out with Kazan."

Background

Asked how he happened to turn to acting,

Dean hoisted a jodhpur over one knee and lit a cigarette. "It was an accident, although I've been involved in some kind of theatrical function or other since I was a child—in school, music, athletics." He rose and began pacing the room. The words came slowly and carefully. "To me acting is the most logical way for people's neuroses to manifest themselves. To my way of thinking, an actor's course is set even before he's out of the cradle."

An only child of non-professionals, Dean was raised by an aunt and uncle in Fairmount, Ind. "My father was a farmer, but he did have this remarkable adeptness with his hands," he said, flexing his own. "Whatever abilities I may have crystallized there in high school, when I was trying to prove something to myself—that I could do it, I suppose. One of my teachers was a frustrated actress. Through her I entered and won a state oratorical dramatic contest, reciting a Dickens piece called 'The Madman.' What's it about? About this real gone cat," he chanted, "who knocks off several people. It also begins with a scream," he remembered casually. "I really woke up those judges."

"All these things," he went on, "were good discipline and experience for me. After graduation, I went to live with my father in Los Angeles—Mother had died when I was a kid—and just for the hell of it, signed up for a pre-law course at U.C.L.A. That did call for a certain knowledge of histrionics. I even joined a fraternity on the campus, but I busted a couple of guys in the nose and got myself kicked out. I wasn't happy in law, either.

"Then I tried my luck in pictures, contacted an agent, got some small parts in things like 'Has Anybody Seen My Gal?,' a Korean war film, 'Fixed Bayonets,' and one TV play.

"I came here at the suggestion of Jimmy Whitmore, a fine actor and a good boy, a real New York boy, who wasn't too happy out at Metro." For what he learned at the Actors' Studio, while edging into prominence on television and in his Broadway bow, "See the Jaguar," Dean pointedly credits director Lee Strasberg, "an incredible man, a walking encyclopedia, with fantastic insight."

Would he compare the stage and screen media? "As of now, I don't consider myself as specifically belonging to either. The cinema is a very truthful medium because the camera doesn't let you get away with anything. On stage, you can even loaf a little, if you're so inclined. Technique, on the other hand, is more important. My aim, my real goal, is to achieve something I call camera-functioning on the stage.

Defense

"Not that I'm down on Hollywood. Take pictures like 'The Ox-Bow Incident,' most of the Lubitsch ones. Gadge (Kazan), of course, is one of the best. Then there's George Stevens, the greatest of them all. I'm supposed to do 'Giant' for him. This guy was born with the movies. So real, unassuming. You'll be talking to him, thinking he missed your point, and then—bang!—he has it."

How did his Warner contract read? "Nine films over a six-year period." Story approval? "Contractually, no—emotionally, yes. They can always suspend me. Money isn't one of my worries, not that I have any.

"Don't get me wrong. I'm not one of the wise ones who try to put Hollywood down. It just happens that I fit to cadence and pace better here as far as living goes. New York is vital, above all, fertile. They're a little harder to find, maybe, but out there in Hollywood, behind all that brick and mortar, there are human beings just as sensitive to fertility. The problem for this cat—myself—is not to get lost." Dean's smile spread as far as his lenses.

With the opening of East of Eden, *Jimmy* not only became an
overnight celebrity but also had to assume many of the obliga-
tions and responsibilities that new role implied. Here, Jane
Deacy and an accountant go over business with Jimmy, who
tries to cope, but . . .

. . . finally solves the problem by putting his feet up and going
to sleep.

Jimmy's apartment on Sixty-eighth Street just off Central Park West was small and stateroomlike, on the top floor—probably a maid's room in earlier days. It was crammed with books and records. Jimmy had a need to be surrounded with books, but I'm not sure he was a real reader. As for his interest in music, he once boasted, "I collect everything from twelfth- and thirteenth-century music to the extreme moderns—you know, Schönberg, Berg, Stravinsky. I also like Sinatra's 'Songs for Young Lovers' album."

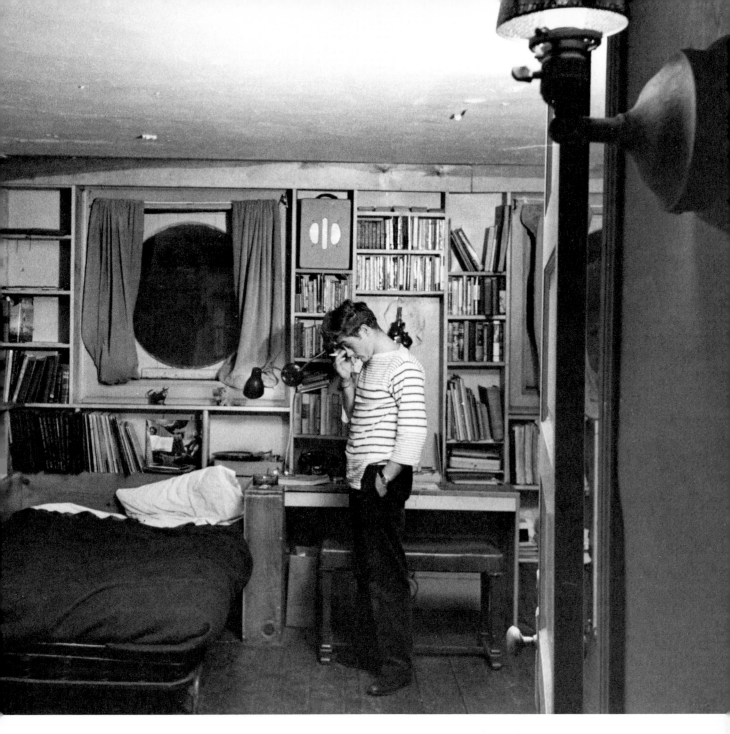

A lot of those books had to do with the theater, of course, but note also Kafka, *I Go Pogo*, *Charlotte's Web*, Thomas Mann's *Death in Venice*, and, lower right, *Los Toros*. A minister in Fairmount had turned him on to bullfighting, an interest reflected as well in the horns and cape on the wall. I don't know whether Jimmy actually ever saw a bullfight, but he played a lot with that cape—fantasized, I suppose. There was something bull-like about Jimmy—testy, untamed, aggressive.

After *East of Eden,* Jimmy had a
long-term nine-picture contract with
Warner. More and more, he saw,
California would necessarily be his
home base. But whenever he could,
he would sneak back to New York,
"to life and the living of it," as he
put it.

One of his great pleasures in New
York was to join Eartha Kitt in one of
her dance classes, or to repair with
her afterward to a bar to talk.

A jam session, New York, spring, 1955.

East of Eden opened in New York at the Astor Theatre, at Forty-fifth and Broadway, on March 10, after a celebrity-studded preview the night before as a benefit for The Actors Studio. But Jimmy was at neither the preview nor the opening. "I'm sorry," he had told Jane Deacy, "I can't handle that scene," and so he boarded a plane for L.A.

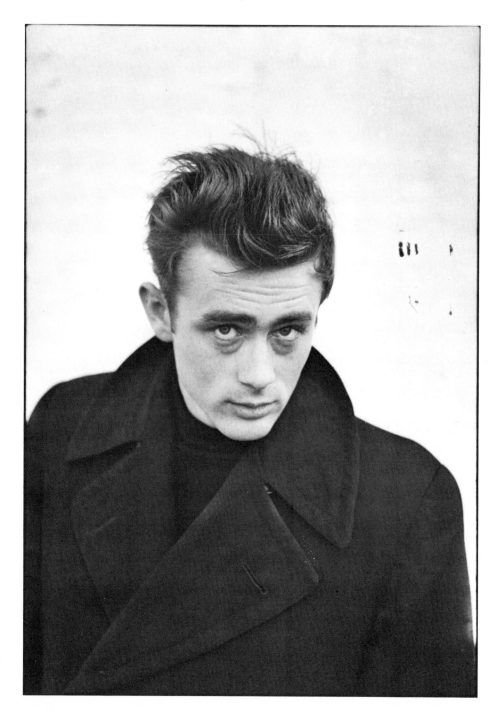

Flying west, on his way to make Rebel Without a Cause.

Hollywood

Back in Hollywood, Jimmy tried to resume old routines, but a combination of his instantaneous fame and his own quirky, complicated personality made that difficult. He still hung out at Googie's, but anonymity, even there, was a thing of the past. Meanwhile he was preparing to film *Rebel Without a Cause*, which Nicholas Ray had persuaded Warner Brothers to make after the property had languished on their shelves for seven years. It was the first movie of the new nine-film contract.

Now poverty was a thing of the past, and with ready cash available, and credit no problem, Jimmy began buying bigger and faster racing cars. He made no bones about it with the studio executives that racing interested him far more than acting, a statement that obviously failed to endear him to them, for two reasons: it was an affront to their corporate and creative dignity; and they felt the damn kid would end up getting hurt, thus endangering their investment on any film in progress. Jimmy's latest acquisition was a four-thousand-dollar Porsche Speedster, which in the spring of 1955 he entered in a race at Palm Springs. He not only won in the amateur class but came in third among the professional drivers, and this only whetted his appetite for more and better races.

He was still insomniac, and night after night he would stay up driving, or drinking, with local cronies or with friends from back home who would come to visit. But no matter how late he stayed up, somehow he usually managed to make it to the set on time. There were exceptions, of course, with which Hollywood legend abounds, but in my experience, when Jimmy held up shooting, or showed up late, it was usually because he was at odds with the studio; it was his way of scoring a point for what he considered to be justice.

James Dean's Hollywood career was brilliant and brief. *East of Eden* opened, as we have seen, in March, 1955. *Rebel* finished shooting in June, 1955. From *Rebel*, Jimmy moved directly to *Giant*, which finished shooting in September of the same year. Before the month was out, Jimmy was dead.

It is interesting to note how various reviewers reacted to James Dean and the three major films that constitute his Hollywood career.

Photographs pages 111, 112, 113, 118, and 119 courtesy Warner Bros..

EAST OF EDEN

"Only a small part of John Steinbeck's *East of Eden* has been used in the motion picture version of it that Elia Kazan has done, and it is questionable whether that part contains the best of the book. . . . But the stubborn fact is that the people who move about in the film are not sufficiently well established to give point to the anguish through which they go, and the demonstrations of their torment are perceptibly stylized and grotesque. Especially is this true of James Dean in the role of Cal. This young actor, who is here doing his first big screen stint, is a mass of histrionic gingerbread. He scuffs his feet, he whirls, he pouts, he sputters, he leans against walls, he rolls his eyes, he swallows his words, he ambles slack-kneed—all like Marlon Brando used to do. Never have we seen a performer so clearly follow another's style. Mr. Kazan should be spanked for permitting him to do such a sophomoric thing. Whatever there might be of reasonable torment in this youngster is buried beneath the clumsy display."

BOSLEY CROWTHER, *The New York Times*, March 10, 1955

"James Dean has been cheapened into a less important sort of myth, but his performance survives with extraordinary force and despair. If ever an errant generation threw up an expression of itself, it was in him: like Cain, he has the look of a fugitive and a vagabond in the earth."

The Observer, August 6, 1961

" . . . nobody can deny Dean's personal achievement in making his role understandable and fascinating."

Look, April 5, 1955

"As Cal, young James Dean . . . is the screen's most sensational male find of the year. . . . His talents are extraordinary."

JESSE ZUNSER, *Cue*, March 12, 1955

" . . . looking again at this first film, I am astounded by his performance. It is even better than I had thought: more truly anguished, more delicately poised between the awkward, sulky scapegoat and the young creature exploding with love. It gives heart and centre to the film. . . . Perhaps as an actor he was lucky to die half-tried, before he could be forced out of his adolescent's shell. In 'East of Eden,' at any rate, his wistful image is undisturbed."

DILYS POWELL, *The New York Times*, August 6, 1961

"It is a tour de force for the director's penchant for hard-hitting forays with life, and as such undoubtedly will be counted among his best screen efforts."

Variety, February 16, 1955

" . . . I was overwhelmed with what they had done. I think it might be the best film I ever saw. I don't think the fact of my having written the book has anything to do with that connection. They have not translated my book. Translations rarely succeed. But they have taken theme and story and set them down in a different medium. What I saw was familiar and true but fresh and new to me. It is a fine thing and I am grateful."

JOHN STEINBECK, New York Herald-Tribune, March 6, 1955

"Jimmy wasn't easy, because it was all new to him. But with affection and patience he got awfully good. God, he gave everything he had. There wasn't anything he held back."

ELIA KAZAN

"Dean was an individualist, an original, and anyone who came in contact with him felt it."

CHRISTINE WHITE

REBEL WITHOUT A CAUSE

"The movie is written and acted so ineptly, directed so sluggishly, that all names but one will be omitted here. The exception is Dean, the gifted young actor who was killed last month. His rare talent and appealing personality even shine through this turgid melodrama."

WILLIAM ZINSSER, New York *Herald-Tribune*, October, 1955

"The late James Dean reveals completely the talent latent in his *East of Eden* performance. As a new unwilling member of the gang, a boy who recognised more clearly than any of the others his need for help, he projects the wildness, the torment and the crude tenderness of a restless generation. Gone are the Brando mannerisms, gone too the obvious Kazan touch. He stands as a remarkable talent; and he was cut down, it would seem, by the very passions he exposes so tellingly in this strange and forceful picture."

ARTHUR KNIGHT, *Saturday Review*

"The performance of the star, James Dean, will excite discussion, especially in connection with the irony of his own recent crash death under real-life conditions of recklessness, which form a press agent frame as the picture goes into release. In *East of Eden* under Elia Kazan's direction the twenty-four-year-old actor was widely thought to be doing a Marlon Brando. But freed from Kazan's evaluations of character this resemblance vanishes. Almost free of mannerisms under Ray's pacing, Dean is very effective as a boy groping for adjustment to people. As a farewell performance he leaves behind, with this film, genuine artistic regret, for here was a talent which might have touched the heights."

Variety

GIANT

" . . . James [Dean's] legend is certainly going to be enhanced by his portrayal of a sullen, swaggering ranch hand who overnight becomes an oil millionaire . . . . 'Giant' can be numbing at times, but through its tremendous variety and vividness, as well as through its sheer weight, it turns into a pile-driver of a picture. . . . But it is James Dean who gives the most striking performance and creates in Jett Rink the most memorable character in 'Giant'. . . . "his depiction of the amoral, reckless, animal-like young ranch hand will not only excite his admirers to frenzy, it will make the most sedate onlooker understand why a James Dean cult ever came into existence."

HERBERT KUPFERBERG, The New York Times, October 11, 1956

"In mood, in movement, 'Giant' is something the film colony often claims but seldom achieves: an epic. . . . James Dean, who was killed in a sportscar crash two weeks after his last scene in 'Giant' was shot, in this film clearly shows for the first (and fatefully the last) time what his admirers always said he had: a streak of genius."

Time, October, 1956

"Jimmy was the most creative person I ever knew, and he was twenty years ahead of his time."

DENNIS HOPPER, 1955

"Jimmy was the runt in the litter of thoroughbreds. You could feel the loneliness beating out of him, and it hit you like a wave."

MERCEDES MCCAMBRIDGE, during the shooting of Giant

"James Dean is utterly winning one moment, obnoxious the rest."

EDNA FERBER, author of Giant

"Jimmy's proud to be an actor, don't ever doubt that. But it's not for the fame, the glamour, the money. It's the sense of achievement, the thrill of doing a good job."

NATALIE WOOD, *Photoplay*, November, 1955

120

"I was in incredible awe of him in many ways. . . . At times I was envious of his aura. . . . I was fascinated by him. . . . [James Dean wasn't] vain. . . . I don't think he knew how good he was."

SAL MINEO to Derek Marlowe, *New York*, November 8, 1976

Epilogue

"If a choice is in order—I'd rather have people hiss than yawn. Any public figure sets himself up as a target and that is the chance he takes. Most of us have more than one choice and I chose to be what I am, rather than remain a farm boy back in Indiana. . . . Despite endless odds and issues along the way, I've never regretted it."

JAMES DEAN

124

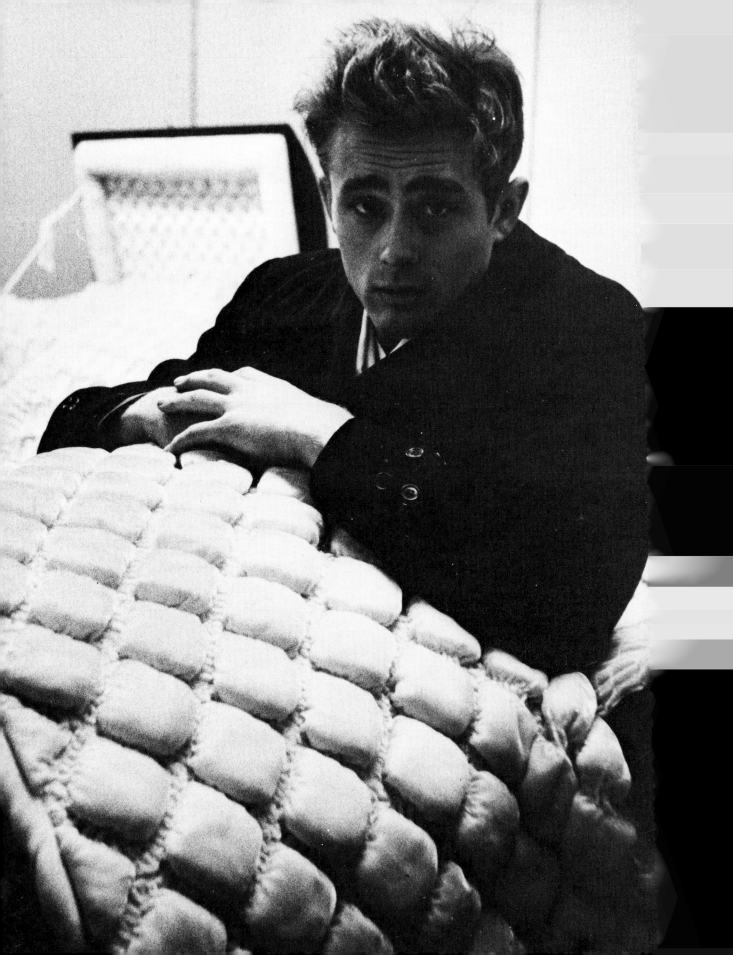

Fairmount, Indiana
September, 1978

Amid a rising ground fog the
gravestone stands. Twin bushes
weakly guard the scarred memorial.
Desperate fans have chipped at his
name, leaving barely discernible
letters.
The surrounding fields of corn and
wheat contract each year where
mobile homes abound. In death's
beauty the autumn leaves lie, mov-
ing only when hurled by the speed
of a passing motorcycle.
The Fairmount of today, like most
rural settings, straddles life and
death proportionately. The folks
perceive James Byron Dean as,
simply, "one of that unusual crop of
the fifties."

"There really isn't an opportunity for greatness in this world. We are impaled on a crock of conditioning. A fish that is in water has no choice that he is. Genius would have it that he swim in sand. . . . We are fish and we drown."

JAMES DEAN